Follow the Laugh on the Path (Book 2)

Bye-Bye, Why! (Book 3)

Getting Down in Sound Town (Book 4)

No part of this publication may be reproduced, distributed, or transmitted in any form or by any means, including photocopying, recording, or other electronic or mechanical methods, without the prior written permission of the publisher, except in the case of brief quotations embodied in critical reviews and certain other noncommercial uses permitted by copyright law. For permission requests, write to the publisher, addressed "Attention: Permissions Coordinator," at the address below:

Robateau & Associates, 78 Ryerson Street, Brooklyn, New York 11205

Addi-Boo Books

Printed by Createspace.com

Text copyright © S. Emmanuel Epps & Lisa Robateau, M.S. CCC-SLP, 2013

Illustrations copyright © Brett Burbridge, 2013

ISBN 978-0-9911410-0-5

All Rights Reserved.

Summary: Young learners sharpen their minds by playing a critical thinking game, learning through colors patterns, analogies, and rhymes.

Manufactured in the United States of America

Dedication

For Susie, Timothy, Lillie and Addison - s.e.

To John, Pablo, and all those that make children feel special - l.r.

"Every man can, if he so desires,
become the sculptor of his own brain."

Professor Santiago Ramon Y. Cajal, Spanish neuroscientist
and winner of the 1906 Nobel Prize in medicine

S. EMMANUEL EPPS

LISA ROBATEAU, M.S. CCC-SLP

ADDI-BOO BOOKS

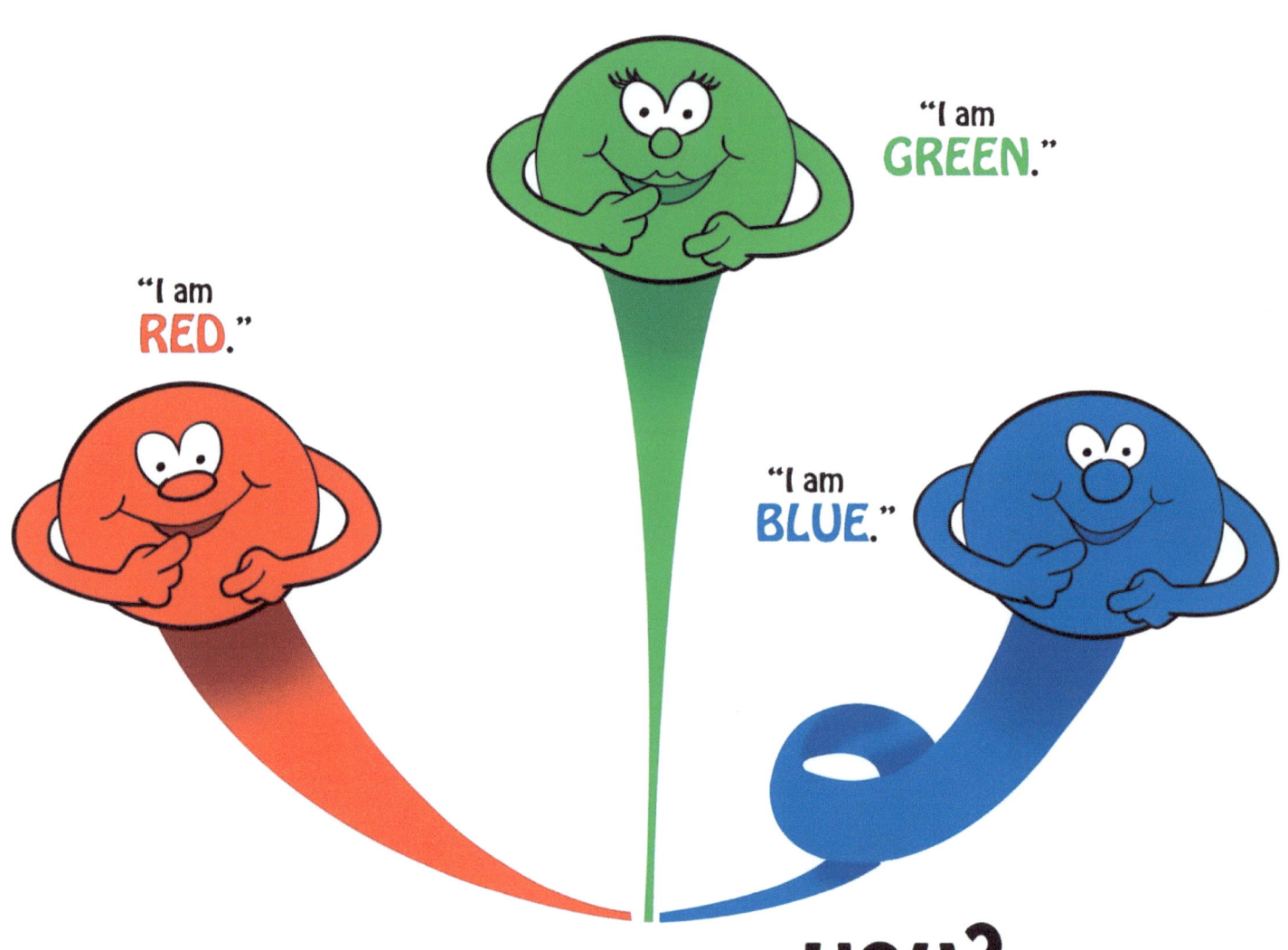

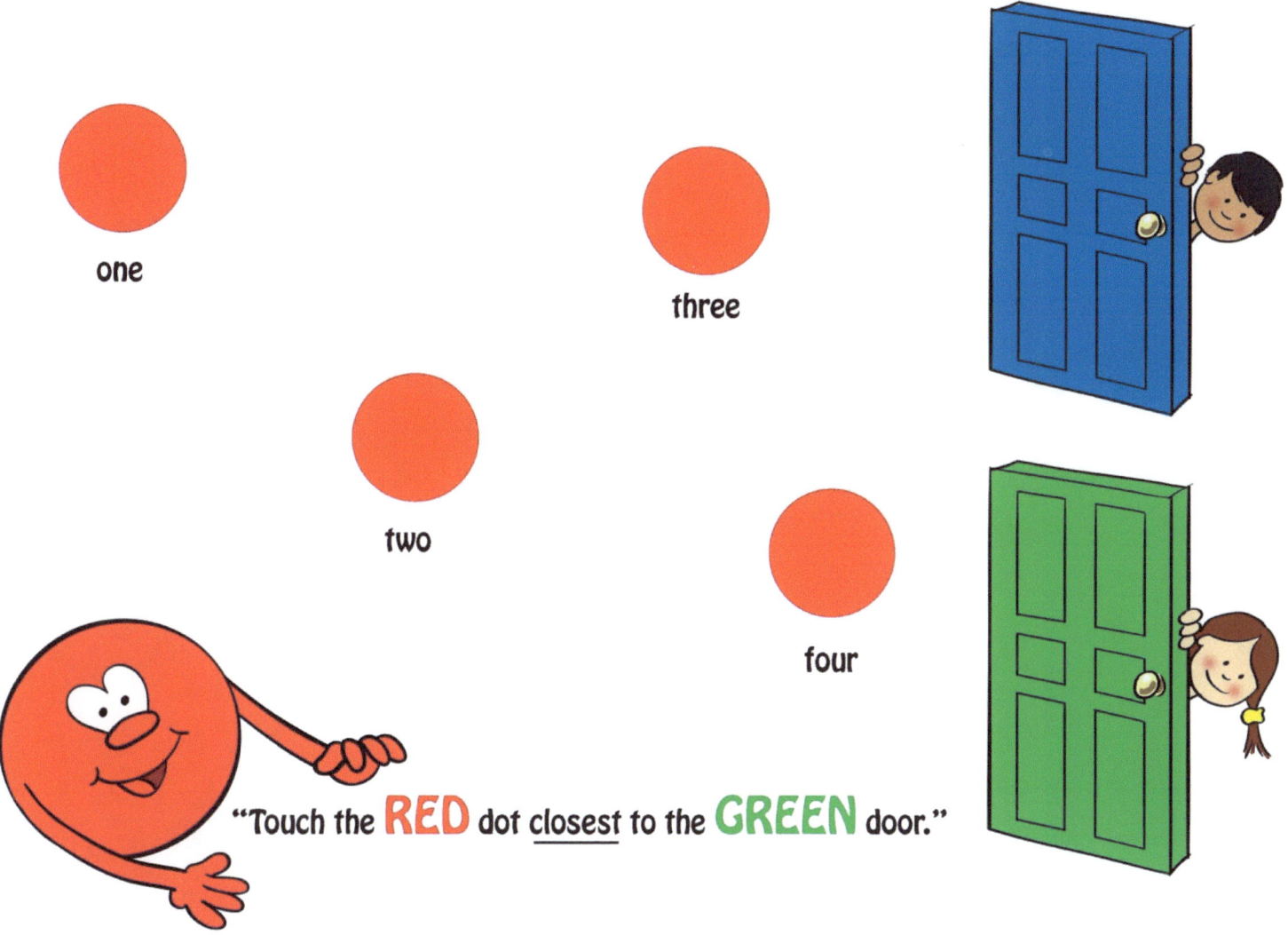

Knock, knock!
Who's there?
"It's me – **GREEN** square."

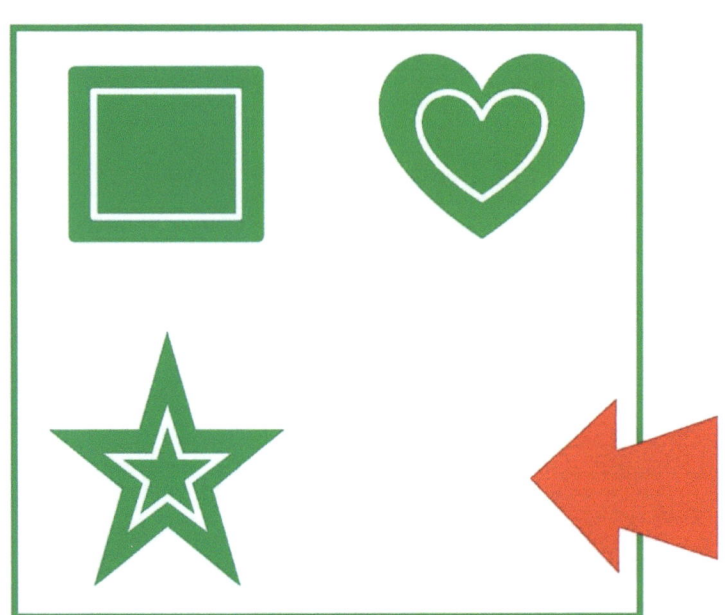

A shape is missing. Which one should go there?

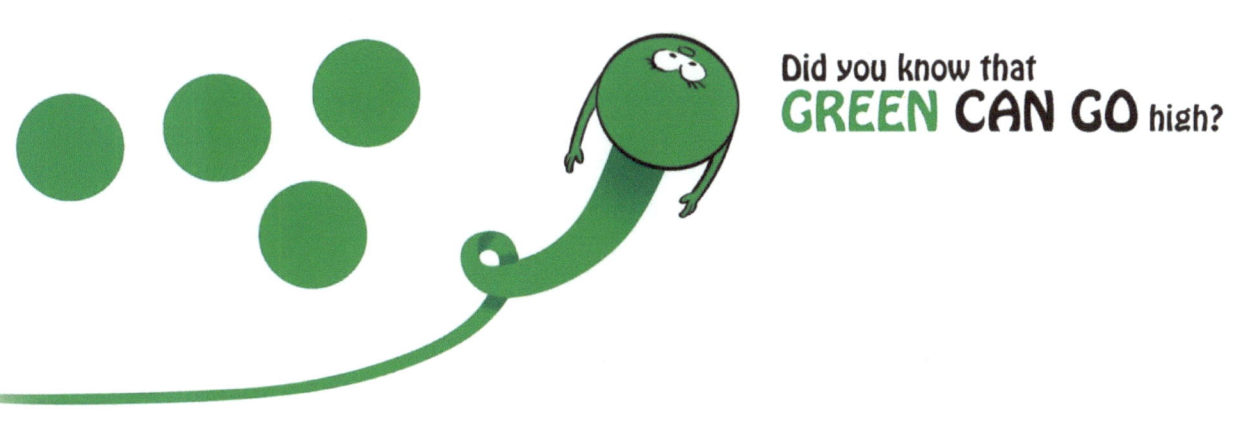

Did you know that **GREEN CAN GO** high?

And **GREEN CAN GO** low?

THESE GREENS are lost.
Where should they go?

"Yes, yes, yes!
We put things where they belong.
Will you help us.
Because something here is **wrong**."

And you are so bright.
You can help make it right.

And then sing, sing, sing
Your favorite song.

Look! Your Song made FOUR DOTS TURN BLUE.

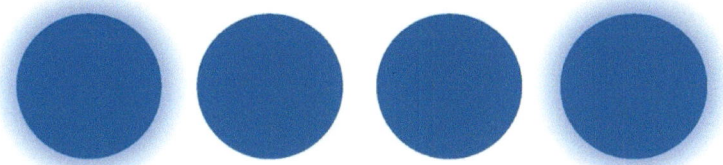

AND THESE FOUR DOTS TURNED BLUE.

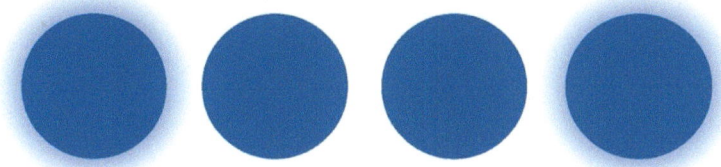

We need two dots here.

Pick two from this group.

What a good job!
You are sooooo smart!

But the **DOTS** are in pieces,
who's missing a part?

If it's **RED**, clap once.

If it's **GREEN**, clap twice.

If it's **BLUE**, clap three times
and then wink your eye.

Whew, YOU did it! **BLUE** IS OKAY!
FOR SUCH A GREAT JOB
SAY "HEY! HEY! HEY! HEY!"

NOW **RED** IS A FISH
THAT SWIMS IN THE SEA.
Three fish are different.
Can you find them for me?

WOW, You're Good!
There's nothing you missed.
You are soooo smart.
I know you know this.

A **RED** bird

a **RED** feather

they DO go together

what two of these **GREEN** things goes best with each other?

WOW, You're doing great!
You just can't miss.
From small to big the better things get.

So choose one worm
Who's the right size
to eat this.

Yummy, Yummy, Yum.
We're having so much fun.
BLUE feels like playing,
playing the drum.

So help **BLUE'S** drum
Stay on beat.

Should we clap our hands here or stomp our feet?

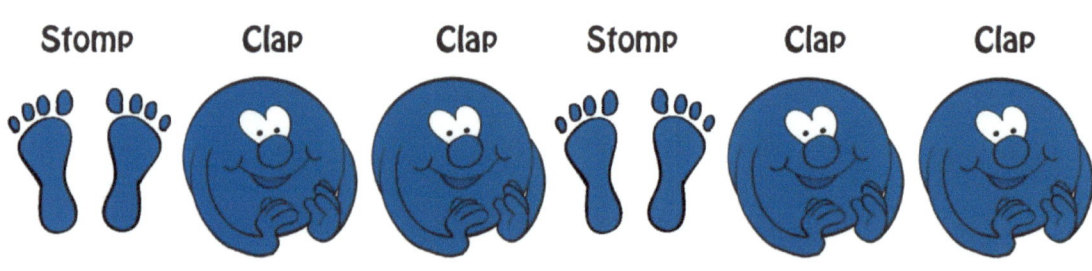

Stomp   Clap   Clap   Stomp   Clap   Clap

WOW, You know a lot. More than we thought...
But can you please tell us
What goes in the **RED** box?

A car,   clothes,   spider web   or rocks?

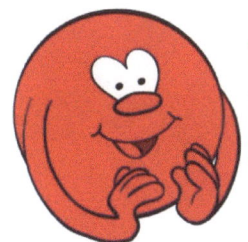

You're right again!
Those things do belong in the **RED** box.
Shirt, pants - and even **GREEN** socks.

You are amazing!
You're good at this game.
But before we say goodbye,
What picture goes in this frame?

Choose from these
and then spell and scream
your name!

Hey, you're good
And this game was fun.
RED, **BLUE**, and **GREEN** are happy you've won.

For now, we are done.
We are done having fun.
You did a great job.
You finished book one.

With each page of our game
Your brain got better.
We know one thing,
"You" and **"Special"** go together.

Glossary of Terms

Common Core State Standard Initiative – Common Core State Standard Initiative refers to a educational initiative in the U.S. that aims to indicate precisely the reading and math goals of K-12 students at each grade level.

Neuroplasticity – Neuroplasticity refers to the idea that the pathways and connections in our brains can be impacted and changed by external factors, from learning something new to our brains responding to injury.

Pattern Completion - Pattern completion is a learning task that refers to our brain's ability to detect regularities in a group and to predict one part of a sequence in a group when given other parts of the sequence in a group. This skill is necessary for phonological awareness.

Reasoning by Analogy – Reasoning by analogy is a learning task that refers to our brain's ability to recognize logical relationships between things. This skill is necessary for language acquisition.

Working Memory – Working memory refers to our brain's ability to temporarily store and manage information for recall in order to complete complex tasks like comprehension.

To learn more, visit www.robateauspeech.com
or email info@robateauspeech.com

Bubble Brain Workout Questions

1) Which one of these words DOES NOT belong? Say each word AND listen carefully.
   - BLUE
   - SHOE
   - OUCH
   - NEW
   - YOU

2) Say each letter in each word. Match the "short" word with the "long" word.

Short	Long
Big	Million
Story	Bigger
Lion	History

3) Count the letters in each word. Find the third letter in each word and then tell us what letter we need to complete this word:

TON_UE

   - Egg
   - Sugar
   - Bag

4) Does the word TISSUE belong in group #1 or group #2? Please, put the word TISSUE where it belongs.

<u>Group #1</u>
Potty
Bathtub
Mirror
Toothbrush

<u>Group #2</u>
Dish
Fork
Cereal
Oven

5) The Letter "D" is missing her little friends. How many friends is the letter "D" missing?

Aa   Bbb   Cccc   D_____

6) We need clothes. Please show us what clothes goes on each body part.

<u>Body Parts</u>
Hands
Neck
Head
Feet
Legs

<u>Clothes</u>
Hat
Pants
Shoes
Scarf
Gloves

About Lisa Robateau

Lisa Robateau, M.S. CCC-SLP, is the President of Robateau & Associates, a neuroscience-based speech-language pathology provider. Lisa Robateau has merged evidence-based techniques, along with the latest technological developments and research in neuroscience, to improve the communicative and cognitive performance of children. For 20 years, Lisa has worked with all types of children, from high-performers to those with ADD/ADHD, from speech delays to sports-related traumatic brain injuries. Lisa is a member of the New York Junior League, the Union League of Chicago, and lives in Brooklyn, New York.

About S. Emmanuel Epps

S. Emmanuel Epps, a Higher Education Officer at the City University of New York, no stranger to high-level gifted thinking, demonstrated math aptitude in 7th grade at the level of a high school senior and reading aptitude at the level of a college freshman. Trained at Morehouse College and Union Theological Seminary, an affiliate of Columbia University, Epps trains students in critical thinking strategies.

www.ingramcontent.com/pod-product-compliance
Lightning Source LLC
Chambersburg PA
CBHW041539040426
42446CB00002B/162